CRAVING
WATER

CRAVING WATER

POEMS OF ORDINARY LIFE
IN A NORTHWEST VILLAGE

MARY LOU SANELLI

PLEASURE BOAT STUDIO:
A LITERARY PRESS

Craving Water: Poems of Ordinary Life in a Northwest Village

By Mary Lou Sanelli

Sanelli, Mary Lou
Craving Water: Poems of Ordinary Life in a Northwest Village
ISBN: 1-929355-19-X

FIRST PRINTING
Library of Congress Control Number: 2004092920

Design and Composition by Diane Rigoli,
Rigoli Artstudio, San Francisco, www.rigoliartstudio.com

Paintings by Diane Ainsworth

PRINTED IN CANADA

PUBLISHED BY
Pleasure Boat Studio: A Literary Press
201 W. 89th Street, #6F
New York, NY 10024

Tel: 212-362-8563
Fax: 888-810-5308
Email: pleasboat@nyc.rr.com
URL: www.pbstudio.com

ACKNOWLEDGMENTS:

Poems in this collection have previously appeared in:

An Anthology of Contemporary Western Women Writers, Volumes I & II (Houghton Mifflin, 2002 & 2004); The Seattle Review; Art Access; Crab Creek Review; Room of One's Own; The Temple; Exhibition; Spindrift; Raven Chronicles; Raven Chronicles: South Sound Edition; Synapse; The Bisbee News; Explorations: The University of Alaska; Arnazella; Lit Rag; National League of American Pen Women; Windfall; Padilla Bay Poets Anthology; Arbitus; Vigilance; The Jefferson County Leader; Between the Lines; Skagit River Poetry Anthology; Jack Straw Writers Project Chapbook; Tidepools: Peninsula College Anthology; In Praise of Fertile Land: An Anthology; Monotaur Press; Cranky; Stringtown.

Poems from this manuscript were a 2003 finalist for the Lois Cranston Memorial Poetry Prize, Calyx Press.

My deepest gratitude to Jim Farmer & Steve Corra of the Port Townsend Parks Department for supporting my work and allowing part of an Artist Trust GAP Grant to be used to install a poetry plaque in three of Port Townsend's city parks: *Two Women on the Belltower Bench, The Ferry,* and *July Morning, Chetzemoka Park.*

I wish to thank The Julia & David White Artist's Colony in Costa Rica for a writing residency where many of these poems were completed.

Special thanks are due to Jack Estes, my editor & publisher, who patiently helps to structure my words. His belief in my work, intelligence, honest critiques, and generosity have led me along.

Grateful thanks to my supportive women friends, who enrich my life in at least a zillion ways.

And particularly to my husband Larry, for support, for steady, solid love, for all.

This book is dedicated
to Port Townsend, Washington.
My home town.

I am eternally grateful to live in a place where I can walk
to get my daily business done.

May it continue to evolve
and transcend.
Just like it's people.

TABLE OF CONTENTS

II

*"Don't you realize that the sea is the home of water?
All water is off on a journey unless it is in the sea, and it
is homesick, and bound to make its way home someday."*

— ZORA NEALE HURSTON

AN INTRODUCTION TO

CRAVING WATER:
POEMS OF ORDINARY LIFE
IN A NORTHWEST VILLAGE

I wrote the poem, "This Fact of Water," one drizzly day in late August, an afternoon fading full-tilt into fall. Each year, during this change of season, I remind myself I *can* cope with the gray skies ever-present in the months to come. That water is our salvation. Our lifeline. That the most common and dangerous hunger in humans is the desire to control. Because when I step outside and inhale that first whiff of autumn after too-short a summer, I am thrown into a state of *wanting* to control...at least the weather. Or the role it will play in my life. But what I crave is to be at peace with it.

So, after the inaugural "water" poem emerged, this manuscript began to grow, not incessant in its seeking but patient, allowing me to evolve at my own pace. And through the process, over a decade of writing and rewriting, I tried to balance the sun-lover inside me with an appreciation of the climate I make my home in. Until I felt glad about the wind and rain. Or, glad-ish. Which, in turn, moved me closer to the life I want to live. Not one of monotony. But an aliveness plump with appreciation. And in all fairness, I could not do this without proper tribute to water. Water in all its diversity. Of a sensual nature that spills softly. And a different sort: the hard-nosed, down-to-earth reality of pain and loss.

The short of it is: The more I examine the essentiality of water, the more I understand how every state of mind and body exists wholly because of it. It seems so obvious, but I had to double dare myself to accept it. And who knows, maybe someday I'll come to love the rainy-gray. It may be a matter of waiting for awareness to age gracefully into awe.

But, I admit, there are times I need to flee to the southwestern desert. Or to Mexico. Hawaii. Florida. Any cheap flight will do. To wake to the sound of doves cooing and sun streaming in till I'm oblivious to gray skies left behind.

So, I include a few beach and desert poems in the mix because this collection, in a sense, is me. The "me" needing to get along with all the parts of myself. The "me" needing breaks in routine and weather, for reflection, for insight, for my very well-being.

THIS FACT OF WATER

More than half our body weight
is pure water. We soak up our living with cells
wide open.

Now, think of nothing
getting past this fact of water,
this way of things. Especially here
in a northeast corner of a Northwest peninsula
where moisture seeps
until fertileness astonishes the eyes, even faces
of stones quicken the senses as the slight weight of moss
melts in your hand.

It is not so much she doesn't believe
my need to praise water
as a challenge to my convictions
when Sensibility summons her lecture

from a well-worn perch on my shoulder:
Remember what death says, she says,
if water is relinquished, life exhales
but does not take a breath.

What I thought: My appreciation of gray skies
doesn't keep well.

What I said: I'm grateful your truths come easy
as weeds from the ground.

Without rain we are the airy bloom
cast in a paperweight, ash beneath a bonfire.

And to be certain I GET IT she adds
a few certainties which affirm life
according to her, a woman confident,
accomplished, at peace in this world.

Without water we are the fruit stand
buckled over at the edge of Sequim
day after the plywood vanished
along with any sign
of its past.

And, there is no shade
of distinction between a fruit stand
and you.

I

"In everyday life, reality is lesson enough."

— JANE O'REILLY

CRAVING WATER

One day I *will* move to the desert
with two ballet hips stiff
as the lawn I'll refuse to water.

Under a ceiling fan and flat blue sky, I'll paint
my toenails terra-cotta-pink and reminisce
about the first days of spring on Puget Sound,
weightiness to the air as if the surface of water waits
to slide over an edge. How I broke
trail to the lagoon and stood, mud up to my instep,
to watch a heron flap its wings: two blue awnings
seeping wet.

The air, dry as wicker, will know nothing
of my past, but loosen my bones so I can dance
a two-step now and then, smell of sagebrush and pitch
itself on even plots of memory till I recall
how someone restless lived
inside my skin all those silver days
when clouds moved in to hover if any sun
dared to linger at my door like a sweetheart.

I'll inform my new neighbors
whose weathered skin wrinkles in folds
that when wind raged off the Pacific and trees
leaned into each other like mourners, I'd grow sluggish
as the cliff they clung to
disintegrating into sand.

Aaah, but in my tile-floored kitchen, I'll look down
at prickly pears left to peel, and back

without regret at the fact that nothing kept me writing
like sky dark as my eyes and hair. Or connected me,
was the tendon replacing outsideness, things I wanted
to do on a bicycle
when summer fueled the air with warmth.

And, I'll think back to when nearly August
meant nearly fall
and the urge to weep would come over me.
How I'd walk outside to save
myself from my own mind, and rediscover how
much I craved the moist smell of grass
renewing its roots, rain that took me seriously
apart as I dug in toward the center of my life
a word at a time.

EVE'S WARNING

New Year's Eve.
We play Rummy 500
knowing we'll never stay awake till midnight,
only a run of pairs on the bar between us.

Dealing the next round,
Eve warns that if I'm not attentive,
my love life will wither like the weight of a rose
pressed under glass.

Her words are huge and glaring: sun
rising on the desert in summer.

Guilt burrows through me.
I lose the game trailing by hundreds.

I walk home to open
champagne and myself, offer both
and make love the way we did
that first night in our young world,
sinking into sleeping bags in the back of a van,
fumbling for one more way to feel
pleasure enough. Desire rolling us together, aching to come
out both sides. Kisses that would burn
through my lips and cremate my skull
if they took a savage form.

Now, like a cat, I claim the warmest plot of bed
until the moon recedes, leaving no light
but a flash as his car approaches.

I sit up, intent on not holding back
sounds I want to utter
slowly, sounds that may seem alien,
not of my making
yet as honed and to the point
as a ray of light or a dart
slicing its metal way
through air.

THE GENE

I drive to the clinic
on the last day of May
when June moves in so moist and leafy
it's hard to imagine half of our state
not shrouded in gray
but glowing in light
east of the mountains
where clouds taper off and all
blue begins.

In the waiting room two flies probe a lamp
echoing the fear buzzing through me
bleak as the freeway I drove to get here
or these sterile white walls.

I swat them. Twin carcasses.
I had to do it or they would sink
me forever into this flourescent hell.

Maybe I'm too heartless.
Too what-the-hell-there's-no-such-thing-as-karma.

I'm pretty sure I won't be a sliver
more saintlike anytime soon.

I wipe my nose with the back of my sleeve,
gnaw my nails, mouth
words of a song I memorized twenty years past
and haven't heard since. Tears skid my cheek,
sting raw splits on my lip.

Dread heats up, scalds
my inner thermal, gives way to the fact
I can't have this cut from me to stave off fate
like a mole or ovary. *Can I?*

So the question becomes:
How *do* I proceed into the rest of my life
while waiting for a pin-prick sized cell
to sneak up from behind
like a hit man?

THE BIKINI

After walking the beach I recall nothing
but two teenage girls sprawled on a blanket,
another cross-legged between them, limbs glowing
with oil, ponytails with unadulterated sheen.

Girls, I say to the air, *you are lovely
as summer.* As am I

if summer has ever been in her forties
and taken decent care of herself.

Memory is unkind when it recounts
who you no longer are.

Two more steps toward the girls
and I'm near enough
to see, hear, even feel my girlhood
bikini inching up my backside, thumbs yanking elastic
as I run to the edge of Long Island Sound,
toes grazing a tolerantly warm body of sea,
coconut balm smeared on my belly and back,
legs newly shaven so tiny bumps rise
where sweat and salt mix.

I remember two slivers of nylon, lines in the cloth
like an etching. Bust cups I tried to fill with kotex
that, if worn today, a sterling band would pierce
my navel, rose tattoo in the small of my back.
Another ring through my eyebrow, my infected nose.

As I watch
(am I hoping to stare my way into their affections?)
one rearranges her cleavage, unhooks a strap to fuse
a pale band running the width of her back with her whole
life still to come, suddenly all its possibilities so near
I touch one

so that, in spite of her age, we are in sync
briefly, for about the time it takes to run
a comb through *my* hair.

TOOLS OF A BOAT BUILDER
—for Ernie Baird

Tools of his trade:
C-clamps. Come-along. Joiner.
Drill Press. Band saw. Rasp.

Tools for coping:
A form of prayer he calls *letting go.*
Concentration until all but the hull before him
is quashed. To languish in a woman's love,
remember a man must work
for everything, intimacy included,
and that employees won't perform by the book
no matter how many times it's read to them.

Going back four generations, no man
in his family worked with his hands.
As a young man he, too,
favored the academic, opinions
rational, scientific,
polished like holiday silver.

Now, living where the New Age
is pitched like fast food,
he says he still hasn't learned much
of what is true or untrue
other than conflict evolves into strength
when he gets out of his own way.

When he shows me a sloop named for his mother,
a smile rocks him slightly forward then back,
nothing more to say.

Small town
with huge heart. And so they come,
as dreamers do, to reemerge.
So many men
leaving convention behind.
Mindful of each other. Of boats.
Marriages may stagger and fall
but ships forgive neglect
and respond to a place deep in a man
in want of wind, weathered boards, and sails
tearing through steady air.

ONE DUSK IN A PORT TOWNSEND SUMMER

A throb of African drums drifts up
from downtown and there is rhythm
in the air my feet move to as I go about pruning
feeling sort of out of the loop
while friends shake it up on city pier
freeing themselves from the weight
of small town reserve.

This is the hour light dissolves
the garden into something paler.
The look less—oh, I don't know—defined
though each daisy is still its own
star beaming, there for the touching.
Halo on a leggy stem.

In a quieter place next door,
a young man dies in his mother's lap.
Son of my good neighbor.
For months, he's thinned into skeletal weight.
Hope and sadness ghosting about,
circling our adjacent yards
in equal measures.

As others dance
he sinks into arms
of devotion gathered like huge,
soft pillows around him.

Now, other sounds mix with the beat
of whichever festival we keep pace with *this* week:

kids shooting hoops across the street,
ferry whistle warning its exit.

Part of me wants to run downtown
but how can I? Instead,
I transplant a Rosemary bush
from clay pot to earth because, suddenly,
its branches seem to reach out
urgently to me with eyes
on my trowel.

LAKES

Crescent:

Blue like you see
on postcards of Hawaii.
Six-hundred feet deep, surrounded
by beach gravel nowhere
near as smooth as sand.

Above, a mountain reveals itself
as fog burns off before
my very eyes. Chin pointed to its peak,
I shout *Storm King.*
Even my nipples salute.

Gibbs:

Local, slimy swimming hole.
I fear leeches, ticks, all things
lurking in mud. And that my friends will discover
just how little discomfort it takes
to completely unnerve me.

Voices taper off as I swim
to the center where, short of breath,
I tread with razor grass and focus
on a shoreline peopled but unhurried.

Angels in the Valley of Heaven:

High mountain pools clear
as gin I mix with lime.
When I pause, the air is all there is
to hear, as if stunned by its own presence.
Clouds unlock and a sudden glow, golden
over the valley, exposes how lonely I've been.
Not for others. For myself.
I long to break open and taste
my life free of people and sound.

When I stretch my limbs and stand, I could walk
in any direction and be still
far from lost.

MADELINE'S ARCHIVES
—for Madeline DeFrees

When I arrive, your smile is wide
enough to hold the fondness I feel
and I think how rare to receive
a poet's support so frank
it begins at a cellular level.

We walk your yard and I can't decide
if it's sea in the distance
or a miscellany of clouds beyond.
Then I mistake parsley for cilantro
(or was it the other way around?) and laugh
because just last year I wrote a book about gardens.
Ever since, mine is weedy, up for grabs
and I'm losing the vocabulary of plant life
much like I lost my way with sea birds
after my Alaska poems were freed.

For lunch, salmon salad on pita.
Compared to my habit
of hard-boiled egg and tomato
inhaled over the sink, this is a holiday
feast *carte du jour*.

I know the effort of this set table, this readying.
I know a writer prefers solitude, her rituals.

Now, the image of crates
aligned in your basement
filled with a devotion to writing
in an age of pen and paper

lies beneath the surface of my thoughts.
The sight of your life's work
not faded by hindsight
but exact, centered clearly in mind.

Something about the chaos
of words intersecting. All the poems
that occurred in your life.

THE ALOHA LEI SHOP

On Mauna Kea Street you'll want to stand
nose pressed to the window
to watch women string leis by hand,
strands in their laps, heads keeping time
to a tune inaudible to pedestrians, the scene
dreamlike as a Disney movie.

My husband does not know what he wants
other than to please me, is in awe
of the contrast of arms
draped with strands of Plumeria:
star-shapes of white
against skin brown as cider.

Pidgin is a local, chop-chop dialect
of English, Chinese, Japanese, Filipino—
any combination till business is done.

When my husband chooses Jasmine,
scent sweet as shampoo,
one women hovers and shakes
her head *yah, yah, yah,*

floral muumuu swaying
like a huge bouquet
draped over calves
firm as melons fit to burst.

Yah, dat pick much good!
Make wife many, many happy!

STANDING IN LINE AT
ALDRICH'S GROCERY

On a summer morning,
if sun casts its warmth without hesitation,
we may chat up the likeliness
of tomatoes *actually* ripening
or how good it feels to sleep
with windows wide open
while curtains billow the air.

Or else
only a nod
relayed through the line
as we cup cups of coffee
sometimes nothing to say.

Other days, because we share so much: the same friend
whose marriage climbed, peaked, and severed.
The same children springing into the store at noon.
The same neighbor whose cancer rose
and spread like fluid between her limbs...
we *find* a reason
to air confusion, joy, amazement, fear—
especially fear
when it sweeps through the pit of our stomachs

briskly as the wind mounting outside
when fall is fully engaged, forcing us to crouch,
run to our cars, climb in
disheveled, angled

before righting ourselves, our bags
this blustery season, its dim light

lingering over those still inside
moving ahead in line and closer
to revealing some new remnant
or candid glimpse
of our entangled lives.

A MARRIAGE

Fifteen minutes into my morning routine
the phone rings. Outside, spring swells
warm from the earth, the first sprouting
which brings to mind moments of pure joy
I once felt tilling a garden in soil
so gloriously rich, awe spread through me
like current.

But, like years, want moves on.
By winding down the way lust abates
or snaring suddenly—tissue
caught on barbed-wire.

Now, with so much to weed, I'd rather write,
neglecting no part of the query
life is.

It's a friend (I have misgivings about)
calling to say her husband left her
for a tango dancer with red hair and breasts
born of silicone. As if a slap bores through the cable
connecting us, I put my hand to my cheek,
my own loyal marriage unable to console.

When she arrives, her eyes are red
as the marrow in bone.
I've never known her like this.
Normally, we're not candid,
constraint like arms locked across our chests.
Ironically, betrayal is our first setting
for trust.

She tries to rationalize deceit, leans
her body into mine as if impact is a bond
that bears up.

My husband's tears turn
the room to half-mast.
I bypass this moist emotion,
head straight for anger.
Not enragement: a child yelling
I hate you I hate you I hate you
but wrath as what is
honest. There isn't enough anger these days.
Instead, we hush ourselves, pretend,
call it something else.

MOTHER OF TWINS
—for Dianne

She snorkels to fall
beneath the surface of a silent world
where she stands, clumsily, on two rubber fins
till a man's legs, clingy bathing suit,
and cloud of silt swirls past her. She takes comfort
in his self-possession, plunges with abandon,
carves a mean stroke
headfirst toward his body.

She kicks away from the beach,
the agitated foam,
as if there is no reason to return
overhead where a thousand duties wait to consume
her swift as flames erase kindling.

She says these are her thoughts
as sea ripples overhead
and she is alone
finally:

Each night as I descend into my bath,
I clutch my twins
buoyantly in each arm, two tiny mouths
suckling the air
as if the presence of water is still needed
in order to breathe.

Day by day, my heart evolves into one
tough enough to hang
this large a love on.

Four sets of gums pinch my nipples
like kitchen tongs till, painfully,
pleasure rises.

As I pour myself inside them, from my breasts
down, we become
one

where I leave off
and my boys begin.

THE GROUNDS OF
FORT WORDEN

After climbing a column of stairs
that carry me from shore with a chafe
of sand in my boots, I'm at the edge of a cliff
that sloughs its permanence
even as the distance sweeps up
into air, light,
a massive stretch of field
framed by barracks on one side,
a row of officer's houses on the other

with wide front porches
that make me think of southern families:
men drafted off plantations
all those wars ago.
How their hands must have numbed in the wind
kicking up between the concrete bunker
they crouched in
and the sea.

And wives who,
bound by their husband's rank,
must have spent more
than a few long moments watching a subtle, low sun
pose sensuously on the horizon, hypnotic
after months of rain.

But mostly, I think of children
running the grand length of lawn
with kites. Nothing to apprehend
but a string overhead.

No reason not to call this place
      that hides the sun
      that is picked clean of Japanese-Americans
      that is thousands of miles from their grandparents
home.

THE BEACH

The tide is low and the beach
wide enough to walk from town
to the lighthouse. The working lighthouse.
Not the replica, decidedly cute, perched
over town to make you think, "Whoa, there.
Wouldn't it be great to live in a lighthouse!"

All it takes for me to shed
myself is sun pouring down.
If no fog greys the horizon, I see
so clearly it cuts worry down to size.

Up close, trees cling to the hillside
and you can feel the essential grace required
to hold the present in place.

Farther down the beach, a volleyball net
where players lunge for the ball.
One man flops to his knees and howls
with anger. Funny how serious he is about a game
especially with his gray hair and varicose veins.
But I'm not here to denounce the militant traits
of competitive sports because, believe me,
that would not be a poem
but a thesis.

By the pier, children release themselves
into space and when you cross the dock
a rush of shore spills out
crescent-shaped before you.

This is where I want to drop
to the sand and let it hold me, toss
my shoes and run, turn a cart wheel in the surf,
feel nothing but the freedom of doing so
if only there was no one...

no teenagers to make fun of my acrobatics,
dogs eager to sniff my gender, or a gossip
I distrust so solidly, watching
to see if I fall.

SCATTERING PAPPY'S ASHES

In the Dungeness Valley we stand,
weight shifted to one leg
then the other. The air
full of those watery sounds
an irrigation ditch makes
carving its way through earth.

A few of us hold flowers,
a tenderness we carry.

I'm nervous, careless
with what I say, whisper to Pappy's wife
how odd it is no one mentions his name.
Just the same old, same old—kids, rain, trivialities—
still shared by the living in a rural town.

I'd take back those words if I could.
I know when mortality meets us
head-on, it's distraction we seek, reprieve
from the burden of mind loss demands.

Now, into the woods, arm in arm
or singular, path muddy under our feet.

When the ashes are spread, scarred trunks of fir
give voice to a man just as rooted, so engaged
nothing *but* death could stop him.

And so we hold on, balance ourselves
against the resolve of the other.
Our lips curve into smiles

somewhat detached
the way we grin when things
are not once removed from familiarity
but twice.

When the tension finally breaks, we hug
full-on as if Pappy has just been born.

The rest of the afternoon we return
to ourselves, try to get there in body, determined
to put the finishing touches on our own lives.
Not one of us sure how to fill the space
of living, how to let go in the end.

AFTER THE TRANSPLANT

Imagine the wound
the word 'cancer' inflicts
first time said in reference to your body.

One hard 'c.' One soft.
Two rather blah syllables
viselike around you.

How just yesterday
you held a firm place in this world.
The worst of your troubles: the everyday
with its many ways of getting to you.
And now you can't remember
that simple life.

And what if someone else's bone marrow
is all that could save you?

If you are the man I know
embraced his sister, her lean body
trembling as she agreed to a transplant

and after surgery, say six months later
this same man is seen around town
in some smart dress and heels...

we wonder

is it due to the stream
of woman running through him, her supple tissue
spread beneath the pocket

of his skin, one thing
seeming like another
unless you know what roots beneath?

Or, when faced with falling
out of life, do we hold up
a light to what is real and finally
let go of the rest?

THE SCENT

In a restaurant I hear my own
story rise in another woman's voice
and settle into adolescence.
I inhale the father-daughter musk, scent of a female
seeking approval.

Even at this age, its mystery of hormones,
in the presence of my dad I regress
into girlhood, a toddler on all fours,
as far from who I want to be as the span of years
since he called me *belle fiore*.

Since I can remember, I, too,
want to sit with my father,
heads tilted back in laughter. To bask
in pride gleaming like gems in his eyes.
To know what it's like to be free
of this absence in me
filled with the presence of him.

Now, she butters bread,
blow-by-blow strokes, orders more wine.

I examine their half-turned faces.
His, creased and hapless though embryo-exact
to hers in shape.

Because she is unmarried,
because she bears a salary instead of children,
reluctance pinches his lips, the groove
over each eye.

She gazes past her father at me.
Alcohol and proximity
lay way to intimacy. I raise my glass,
toast the space unfilled, the mood
unalive; mouth the words, *I know.*

Gratitude opens her face, her smile
a light falling over the room. I reach out
as if to catch it, a ray
sharp enough to hang my hopes on,
my own want
still a pleat in the air.

MEETING SETH AT
WATERFRONT PIZZA

As the sun climbs to mid-day
we share a beer, gossip
harmless enough.
Nothing too trashy.

In the reserve of our friendship,
releasing ourselves is currency, a silver dollar,
a small worthy thing we hold onto.

When young, he says, he looked to others
to measure his own merits by. To this day,
his self-esteem is nil and I think how hard
it is to pass the past on, its scars.
I want an act of will to swell up
and burst like a blow hole
to liberate his habit of doubt.

When he describes me to me
(a gust of getting things done)
we agree
it's my father's fault, his work ethic
ironlike in me as the pile driver
hammering in the distance,
driving us to drink up, bustle into farewell, return
to various selves, concerns, the push
it takes to earn one's way.

Recently, I lost a friend.
She and I went searching for women
other than ones we'd become.

I think of her while walking with this man,
companion completely. My heart grows
no larger than this.

Once he and I shopped together
hours in artificial light.
He needed shoes, shirt, pants.
Even a tie.

Surrounded by so much to buy,
we grew weary, bickered briefly,
until laughter leaned in, nudged our words,
made ones not exactly kind
kind.

BREAKING WATER

Halfway through lunch
a trickle runs down your thigh, each drop lengthened
and suspended. *I am not ready* is what you think
when it splashes the ankles
you carry like weights.

Nervously, the waitress ushers you,
though you both know sliding your arm through hers
is not even *close* to holding on.
When your feet slip in liquid
pooling the legs of your chair, you are grateful
no one laughs or speaks.

Outside, you look down
at two water-stained shoes and back
at the restaurant because you can't stand
the thought of busboys mopping your fluids
like overturned beer.

At this point, life demands
to retell itself. You lean
against a power pole,
clasp its trunk as if it were human,
a belly offering warmth.

As your child slides into a core
beyond yours, there is no time
to convince the world more of you
needs to dilate than the cervix
that burns clear to your chest.

You remember to breathe
every breath at half speed, to leave
the earth behind, to scroll back to before
pain took such a sharp bite out of your courage.

And to close your eyes, blear
all else, release yourself
in two.

REUNION

Next to me,
my mother reads a romance novel
on a bench in Waikiki,
palm fronds rustling
stiffly overhead, feet
basined in sand.

The book cover
flaunts an open-mouthed woman,
breasts like globes giving way
from a blouse
unbuttoned neck to waist.

I look out to sea,
see cargo ships, kayaks, swimmers
smooth in their stroke, myself
years from now, returning
to this satisfying light that warms
the deepest rifts of my body.

No daughter.
No one who is part of me
and me of her,
looking with disapproval
out the corner of her eye
at books I read

so the mood hanging over us
like a gavel
falls, the rest of the day doomed
as lobsters in a tank, both of us

wondering what might restore us
to the same world
where we are one
sum—mother, daughter, whole
expanded heart
without so much

separateness
marbled in.

PONDERING AT DAWN
IN THE WAKE OF
SEPTEMBER ELEVENTH

Above us, rain drums the skylight.
My husband's hand
rests on the small of my back.
His feet, heat conduits
planted firmly between my calves.

At this hour,
the cage of my chest opens
perfectly raw, truth exposed, echoing
from a place where worry collects.

I am nothing
but afraid of war.
And I have so much faith
in my lack of courage to endure it.
I'm a woman who lives with one man, two cats,
on half a city lot. Yet, it's obvious the world
and every small life like mine
is on the brink.

The moon glows
like china in the otherwise dark.
While more bombs fall on another land,
there is still so much beauty in the world,
even from the warmth of my bed,
so to spare myself the guilt
this inner implosion of truth will take,
I think of smaller things, day-to-dayness:
how young friends try my knowledge on

like clothes, leave me guarded, afraid
to straight talk from a solid place
gathered like weight with the years.

Yet, with older friends, I recoil, come up short
of savvy, weigh in a little naive.

And a friend I drink with
to ease boredom between two
who share only the past. Wine till it stokes us
and we warm to each other.

Another, shallow as a tennis court puddle,
bleached hair brittle as straw, nails like swords
polished to perform. Yet her generosity is alive
as a mother's embrace. When we hug
we know what it is in the pure silence of our arms
that connects us, makes us whole.

That said, I roll over. My husband moans.
My fingers find the gully between spine
and the bone of his hip. His legs curve
to accept my knees, then the whole
soft length of leg. We lie, each a part of the other,
snug as seeds in bread.

Still...this knot in the pit of my stomach
takes leave of my body, winds up
and circles overhead.
I wonder if I *can* be honest
about my view of war, an opinion

I have to make up as I go. For instance,
last night while listening to three women
deliver the Vagina Monologues,
I was told 400,000 women were raped
in this country last year alone.
So now I believe what they believe:
we've been at war all along!

I take my husband's hand, clutch it
in both of mine, wonder if others lie in their beds
looking through a pane of glass,
war-experience nil, but still wanting
out of retaliation, the shame it instills,
as we examine from every angle
our part in all this
like X-rays scan bone.

Denial is not possible.

As I get older and...well...older
I wonder how I will relinquish one
by one as years pass,
each friend, each misgiving,
each war, religion, and culture
I scurry to tutor myself about?

And finally, with grace
if I can summon any,
the very life I had.

LOOKING UP

This morning
a crow rests on the skylight.
Black beak and belly.
Claws clicking glass.

The skylight was a gift from my husband
after every need opened inside me
and tumbled out as I pleaded for life
with more light.

Next day he cut into our roof.

Now there is glass, a clear pane of sky
perfectly centered overhead so air is visible,
heat held tight

so when I try
for sleep, moonlight
throws itself in my direction
sky, sky, sky, all astir
and awake.

The crow squawks, startles me
into reliving the kindness
my husband carved into our ceiling.

His selflessness
dilates my affection, is deeper
than a dozen winters
stacked against me.

I want to say
everything about him
is like this,
altruistic, unlike the self-concern
that is my nature

even when I wish it weren't so.

LEAVING SEATTLE
FOR THE DESERT

I can't think of a good beginning
other than it's August and I don't mind
exhilarating rain, celestial plugs pulled from above.
The overcast, the wind, the rage!

I *do* mind sulking rain. In *summer*.
Relentless, sulking, summer rain.

I envy my friend who swears
clouds step up her appetite
for sex. In this climate
I need to find sun in the garden
of my bed, she warns. If skies close in,
find another way of opening.

Perhaps I do need more time on my knees
in that garden. Yet, all I crave is sky
without movement by way of blue
without end.

I fly to Palm Springs.

When I step from the plane,
my limbs move languidly
already tapped out by heat and I know
why the fare is half-price, why a bargain
is generally not. That'll teach me
for trusting desire.

When twilight finally leaves
me sighing, I watch a man plant trees
to keep a fairway from slipping into sand
before he sweeps the entire green
with a palm frond.

Buenos noches, he says.

Because I ask, I learn he is from Tijuana,
that his wife works in the hotel café
spending hours after breakfast
setting tables for lunch.
No use trying to hide
my leather bag and shoes.

In the pool, a school of aged faces
Maybellined into life.
Before long, thousands more will come, bones aching,
a mile a minute by air when apples begin to fall
up north. And later—white as the teeth we are
born with—snow. Whole cities
slowed by its embrace.

ULTRASOUND
—for Max

Now that you are gloriously rounded,
the weight of your child exposed,
recurring questions surface and break
like waves into fear:
Between us, will a chasm fan out?
You on one side with child, me on the other?

As your belly, stretched for one
more life to lie beneath,
is spread with gel, it startles
you and bothers me
no one in the hospital's orbit
thought to warm the tube.

A bitter, hygienic smell wafts up.
Suddenly, my thighs ache
for no good reason. I knead them
relieved a sensor rolls over your abdomen.
I feared a needle the size of a pen
would need to pierce flesh.

A knot of concern at your side, my eyes
fix on a silent screen.

Fluids rise black. So bladder and belly are dark
bobbing dots no larger than dimes.
Lens zooms in, blur becomes body:
heart pulsing, layers of rib, arms extended
as if to hold our gaze.

Ohmygod! Two legs with a limb
vertical between, erect as a soldier in line.
We grin like voyeurs, drink in the news.
It seems to fill us.

When the monitor dissolves
into static we want our boy back
on our side of life. All of him,
say, in a flannel gown.

As you smooth the printout
like Braille beneath your fingers,
I see he is the reason you live now
as much as the air.

THANKSGIVING ON
MARROWSTONE ISLAND

Why don't we do this more often?
Sit around a fire. Feast on salmon
branded with grill lines, eat oysters
steaming in shells.

Then head for the bluff
to throw stones in the straits.
The point being to aim at one
of two large rocks below.
But really, no point
other than time with friends
until playfulness subdues ambition
in the biggest way.

Missfires *kaplunk* the sea.
By the second round, we're not even trying
to bull's-eye. Comradery is enough.

Back at the house
we stand by the wood stove,
chink glasses together
while worries lose hold and fade
like daylight till we sense
what we fear could go wrong in our lives
is, in all likelihood, worse than what will.

And by letting go, we find something
to cling to, these flames rekindling all we have
meant to each other, comfort that roots itself
till we shine
in one another's care.

Not one of us consciously aware
how good it is to move
into the past
presently tied
together like this.

DISTANCE

—Portal, Arizona

It frees my mind
to drive at a speed like flying,
metal and glass
holding its breath.

I pass a hundred miles of open cattle range
with no sign of water, other than a mirage
unrolling broad as carpet, and sweat
absorbed so quickly it holds no presence.

Another ninety miles and one
speeding ticket from a cop who came up
like a hawk swooping down, the road dead-ends
at a ridge where the air is silent
but for a creek washing over stone.
And birdsong.

When I enter the only café,
a rancher removes his hat,
lays it upside down so as not to crush its brim.
Eight deer paws drilled into the wall
are hooks, the waitress says, for hunters' hats.
I say, *I don't get men who sport-kill the wild,*
thinking we'll share a girl-to-girl moment
but she shrugs, walks away.

I should know by now not to rush intimacy.
But I'm east coast Italian. This far west
my instincts mostly misfire.

Chagrined, I take a seat under a stuffed rattlesnake
dazed and suspended, each year of life
held in the rings of its tail.

Later, back in Bisbee,
a bona fide cowboy buys me a beer
at the Copper Queen and I think, yeah,
I'd like to listen to the story of a man
with gentle blue eyes and spurs on his boots

but I keep my eyes down
because I travel alone and in my experience
men misread this.

WHEN SHE IS NOW A HE
IN A BAR NAMED SIRENS

Every poem takes
place somewhere.

This one in a pub
with friends
close enough to touch. One
looks so butch compared to her recent self
a month ago when I remember
liking her dress, her shoes.

Hey, the bartender says,
your friend has been a man all along.

The impact of his words leaves
the world suspended, surreal,

how it feels during an eclipse
when you try to hold on
as sun lets go.

Now, an oddly familiar man taps my arm.
In his eyes, affection
I appreciate in a crowd, his ease
easing my wobbly way with small talk.

I raise my glass, toast his courage,
drink too much too fast. Another swig
and I think: naive married straight girl
meets transsexual.

I step outside.
The moon rises and sets
the sea aglow. An island
grayed by a bank of fog
awaits the ferry.

I stare at the sand, thankful
for ebb tide, no flooding
or receding. For a pause
before the shift.

SECRET PURPOSE
—for Rachel

On a walk through town,
my right arm looped through your left,
our heads inclined toward words we share
about the winter blues, a certainty in our lives
insistent as will.

I ask about the legitimacy of full spectrum light.
You want to know at what age
do we find a desert home to flee to in winter
until the year we stay through spring,
then each season back to back.
I say by then my tush will have already traveled
down south that far and we laugh
as hard from our mouths as we cry from our eyes.
In the language of emotion we are polyglots.

Together, we clutch at ways to console
our dread of planets revolving, summer unraveling.
Firm as trees, we brace ourselves, give up
our last unsteady leaves, walk on
to the pub to toast our bravado.

One martini into this night
I come full circle. Sharing a drink
like pleasures of all kinds
calls for a certain self-forgetfulness
till truth splashes red
on dull self pity:
My friends are cross threads
I tie myself together with.

Decades deep into our familiarity, our plights,
suddenly means more than any yearning for clear skies.
Because even on the shortest, darkest day of the year,
light is shed between us, specific light
that can extend outward like the spokes of a wheel
and still hold tight.

With this I'm released
into the marvel of the present, the secret purpose
of a moon dog of ice. Its white silence
willing us to need each other
more than before.

THE VIOLIN MAKER
TRAVELS TO BRAZIL

At the mill, trees stack tall
as they recently grew. Slash burns.
Sky glows orange. Ash floats
like thousands of swirling gray moths.

After hours of buying wood
precious as gold, he heads for the hotel
pool where sunbathers lie topless
deaf to his stares.

A stone wall
built to separate poverty from pleasure
is no deterrent for a boy who sprints
to where a watch and wallet lie unwatched
on a vinyl cushion. Clearly he is not personnel
in a coat too tight to button.

This is when the violin maker yells
for a guard who bolts from a dark place
of waiting to where light and scratching
for existence meet. As if so little
is to it, he shoots the boy dead.

Now, violins are hid away, no sound in them
and the maker hasn't slept, is sick with regret.
And when it rains, he says, each drop
spits in his face, unrelenting
as the regret we go over again
as he tries in fits and starts
to clutch his sorrow like a rock in one hand
so he might hurl it and be rid.

Behind him, the moon.
On either side, stars
bright as children's eyes.

We turn our chairs, try to let the night move us
back to when he didn't know guilt so raw
he swears he can smell it, as if some part of his flesh
has gone bad as the self-respect
he says he never gave much thought to
until it was gone.

II

"Write your self's self where it lives."

— ANNE SEXTON

JULY MORNING,
CHETZEMOKA PARK

I rock in the double swing
closest to the sandbox
where moms chat up pre-schools
or the latest movie at *The Rose.*

Meanwhile, morning strolls toward noon.
Soon one woman will brush
sand off her child's backside
and the others will follow suit.

On this green stretch of land
beach-bound, camouflaged in cedar, I sink
into calm even when a woman walks by and throws
a glance that shoots a dagger through my mood.
It's appropriate to say, due to the frankness
of our last bout with words I am cut
from her life but that's another small town poem
entirely.

On a rare day without work,
I lie on my back looking up
at a maze of clouds that give shape
to a puffy clan of faces I try to name.
One looks like my Uncle Pete
morning after a poker game
up there in a sky of double-chins.

This is when it strikes
me there are no words to make this real
more real. When watching the crows

is more than enough effort for one day.
That and giving thanks.

By the gazebo, a friend mows the lawn
and waves because when I think of it
we've know each other a decade now
plus a few years. His presence
comforting as everything
else I've grown used to.

In summer it's easy to resist all I know
of fall, winter, persistent parts of spring.
When sunless skies affirm the truth
of rivers, rain, lakes, and sea.
Where, if a city park could speak she'd say,
Girl, don't whine! Rain is the very reason
I am ravishing as this!

TWO WOMEN ON THE
BELL TOWER BENCH

I arrive at the Bell Tower
and they go on
talking about some silly thing they did
when they were girls. One keeps saying,
remember, remember?

The ferry glides
serenely by, brimming with tourists
gathered on deck for a feast of seeing
the way of our town.

When the other women says,
Oh, I don't know if he ever really loved me...
I turn to go
because he must be her husband.
But the other leans in, caresses her friend's hand,
kisses it lightly, says, *your father loved you,*
and I don't know why I feel relieved
but I do.

After a pause, I walk on.
Their voices follow, especially the laughter
(so elated, so shared) bubbling
with affection, the champagne
of intimacy.

Because of their bond
no loneliness invades my aloneness. I bend
to pick a few daffodil buds
carry them home

and later on my sill
they swell open and beam
like candles.

THE FERRY

We climb to the upper deck
where stars by the zillions are tossed
seeds of light I would peck
at if I could.

Behind, Whidbey Island fades while
Port Townsend is a thousand
lamps swaying before us.

In summer, more people come topside
to be part of a night like this, the moon
not above but right here for the asking.

Mid-sound, a silhouette of Mount Baker,
great active crest ascending a fault
restless as two boys who race by.

One boy tumbles, stops
moving to reassemble his pride, muscles
posed against humiliation. Then he laughs
uncontrollably, *ha ha ho ho he he*
and he is the most lighthearted
I've seen anyone, ever.

I need more child-like reactions
to my falls, more
uncensored releases all-around.
I vow right here on this steel ship
to take more joy in life. Schmalzy words
but I draw them in just the same
so the rest of me might wind around them.

The ferry nudges the dock.
Some of us are home. Others
turn toward the relief map on the wall.
I smile at their huddled enthusiasm, the surge
of fascination we feel when a place is new.

Some days are small
full-size lessons. Tomorrow I'll try
to see nothing
but this green and peopled land
as if I carry a backpack and wide-angle lens.
As if I need a place to stay for the night.

HORIZON AIR, SEATTLE TO PORT ANGELES

Twenty-one seats
counting two for the pilots
and a woman
one row back
in denim pants, denim hat
is rubbing her shins and my shins
hurt because I'm back from San Francisco
all those hills I climbed
in city shoes, in fog

our plane plows on, briefly
clouds cease so our shadow displays itself
T-shaped and passing over soft green slopes in the land
while my husband reads
and holds my hand as my nerves come undone one
synapse at a time
because I fear the sky is not safe
with all its blue below us.

The woman in jeans
asks if I'm OK and I say strange
the way we shake in the belly of this squall

and, later at the gate, a man kisses her
tenderly, rolls her suitcase over blacktop
puddled with rain.

Keys in hand, I release
a lock, my car yawns open,
familiar scents rise up, ones I'm part of

in my metal womb as I drive

miles toward home
past lumber mills in the Port of Angels,
a valley, a strip town, a ridge
of clear-cut exposing the truth
of me, of all writers and readers: the reality
of paper.

NAMING THE BIRDS

Newly arrived from an eastern city,
she takes her bird book to heart
with the passion she recently poured
into stocks, bonds, banks.

I'm grateful for my friend
who says *grosbeak*
as one flies through an awning of poplars so tall
we stroll under a canopy of shade. I'm here
twenty years and know only the ordinary
crow, robin, wren.

She and I leave this place behind
in mind. What we think takes root, grows
huge into small talk: politics, marriage, men
with ponytails hanging gray. How weary
they look gone to seed like that.

I've missed this kind of intensity
meant not to separate but stimulate
for the sake of it. How easy it is
to startle the locals
with our ways and words
without even trying. I tell her last time
I tried, *really really* tried

was at a conference in Seattle
where I sat with a name tag, pinned
between two fishermen, one using the word *cunt*
two, three times in reference to his ex-wife,
bringing back a side of me I'd nearly silenced

since moving to a small town.

What I did was pour
my wine into his crotch,
splashing through hesitation
I would have made a pact with
closer to home, stopping short of doing
what needed doing.

THE POTTER'S SHED
—*Otter Rock, Oregon*

The shed is lined with bags of clay.
Clay before possibilities.
Before technique is crucial and extraneous
at once. Before it's hauled to a gallery
where tourists browse
after peering into *The Devil's Punch Bowl,*
a chiseled hole in rock where waves race through
and recede, wild sea
flying in every direction.

This is what I veer off Highway 101 to see
after slowing to a crawl where a bluff
hangs slack, tree roots exposed
as if a limb had been attached.
For miles disclaimers scar the shoreline
so by the time I reach any sand,
I'm so cautious it's not fun anymore.

I came to this granite coast to write
but edginess fills my room
of contrasts: window shades buckling
like leaves, mattress mushy and damp.

In town, a bearded man talks
to himself, to locals, to me
reluctantly raising my head
because I've been alone for days
and don't mind his baiting my silence.

No way I'll turn back.

I flee over the mountains with sun
rising in my windows. Speed my way
into summer. Leave the potter's shed
to the potter. Bring back of it a glazed-blue cup
and in memory, after I settle back
into routines of doing,

what time
does not chip away.

FAMILY BOND

Husband, wife, daughter
maybe twelve years old. Average
suburban family only more so
as if layers of convention bear weight.

We stay at the same motel, study maps
for pueblos to tour, stare at the sky
from white chairs scored with cigarette burns.

It doesn't take long to see the mother
mistrusts me, my traveling alone.
When I say "hi" to her daughter
she hums a little tune like a man might do
while stalking a dear.
You'd think I'd just stepped
from my pants and made her look.

Ahead, there are hours
to watch my shadow wane over a heart
shaped rock the color of sand. So far from home
it's consoling to see the moon rise
precisely where it should.

Morning. Mother and girl
swim laps in the pool. Dad observes
but does not join in as if the body
of water is theirs alone, much like their laughter
he is left alone to overhear.

When they leave, the woman walks
hand in hand with the girl. Father

a few paces behind. At first they leave
footprints like fresh paint, then
nothing.

In five years, whose palm will this woman grasp
when her daughter leaves to unearth the world
and her husband has forgotten her touch, the muscle
of her tongue? Any spark between them
lying so low
it is

lost.

THE ACTRESS
—for Bonnie

The way you looked up
from the dryer as I came in the door,
your arms full of clothes, *hi*
formed with your mouth
but no sound

the way you dropped your bundle
and took me by the hand

the way you led me to your yard
sunk deep in summer bloom, branching
all angles to the light

the way your kid's tree fort came into view
as more than a clumsy mix of wood and nails
and made me long
to pull myself up by its laddered mane.

I would like to say I came for solace
but, truth is, I didn't.
It's just that soon as I see you,
if any little thing struggles internal,
my guard tumbles down

and from my eyes
whole rivers spill
until laughter lightens me, oh, at least a ton
as we talk on, and on, and on
nodding yes, and no, and yes—a gust of giving
we ride like gulls. How healing

to lie back into what I've needed
all my life to know, trust
warm as a newly ironed shirt.

Perhaps others have known it, felt it
when you're lead on stage
or in a minor role
when motherhood and marriage fray
the edges of your life. Regardless
we fall under your enormous spell
as a light opens for us
and we open to let it in.

NOTES FROM NEW MEXICO

I. Monsoon

Just when the air is parched
as if day is back to back with day,
no cool night between, an urgent flash of light
warns of thunder and there is no end
to how frail I feel in its wake.

Then rain in arrows until,
like nervous fingers, a soft tapping.

This is the hour couples make love,
kids stomp and slide,
the old feel a sway in their joints.

I string laundry
like flimsy ghosts through the yard.
In minutes it's dry. I long to tell someone.
Someone from Seattle.

And my hair. Without humidity
it falls in long, dark wings. Like Cher's.
When I think of the hours I've spent with a flat-iron
suppressing each kink and curl.

II. Cowboy

I stare at spurs like chimes when he walks.
At leather-lined thighs and hat
size of a satellite dish.

His driveway, thirty miles long,
is splayed between two ranches, each larger
than the state of Rhode Island.

III. Pacific Northwest

I remind myself the same sun rises over land
a thousand miles north of here
where sea is mother at the core of our lives.

No one would guess by what I write
that I miss the green
wads of moss, the swollen skies.

Yet I do.

THE VIEW

Your children sleep and you
drift downstream
light as balsa.

The river widens
as you remember
no matter how many
you are filtered through by day, you—
family of one—are separate.

Kids need plenty.
And, in spite of how vast your fatigue,
you work to provide.

Time whirls, cuts up your days.
Bits scatter here and there. By evening
you salvage the excess, any scrap
large enough to wad.

You don't believe
a male god has the strength
to nurture this world. Not of muscle
but mind.
How many men do you know, you ask,
who are kind in the hub of chaos, patient
as the shipwreck of family life
keels over in the sand?

On one of those insufferable days,
when you need to cry a good long cry or else
get angry, you walk to the summit of town,

to the rim of the high-school tennis court
where rain pools, shimmers like ice.
The view of our village
haloed between sea and sky
turns your troubles into the tiniest thing, softens the fear
that binds your shoulders into stone. Slowly

sureness returns, enfolds you whole
and near as the roof of your car, is a feather
quilt you lie under.

A WEDDING DRESS

On Taylor Street,
above a chic kitchen store
and community bulletin board
where dozens of flyers fight
haphazardly for space,
there is a sewing salon I peer into
from my own studio across the way.

Below, a steady flow of tourists. Above,
clouds absorb the warmth
rousing the earthy smell of mud flats
and a city of musty buildings
decomposing.

In the salon
a woman tries on a wedding gown
with friends standing intimately close
throughout the fitting.

I am touched by the past becoming future
from this perspective, by those
who deepen their lives with casual touches.

This is the kind of celebration
a wedding dress brings to a place,
an afternoon, the whole world
waiting for moments like this

whether I am one with the gown
or just watching, not a part, just watching
from a neighboring window, the sun's soft glow

rippling antique glass, the laughter
I see but cannot hear

a gift I give myself
before easing off the sill and returning
to the barre and mirrored silence
a dancer knows.

ITS VERY AIR

It's the kind of morning I hold coffee
as if a treasure before me, walk my yard
to praise its imperfections: spindly try
at a lawn, mole holes gnarled as potatoes.

I may even run, caffeine induced,
hellbent to the bluff, breathless because I race
like a kid laughing up at the sun
struck fullness of sky.

Or gamble for clear skies
renewed tomorrow. Head for the Pacific.
Throw a beat-up tent in the car,
logs from a pile slumped against the house
for the imminent splitting I don't dare mention
because I want this weather committed to memory
free of what will come
gusting later. To grasp its very air
tightly round me as the shawl I wear.

Please
allow me to spill just one
more summer theme at your feet:
What sees me through
winter (as much as warm socks and traveling
tropical) is the steamy work of canning peaches
until each Ball jar is poised,
a still life.

So when an ice storm swerves traffic,
power lines in frozen sheathes

snap and fry, I feast on fruit. Syrup
straight up. Glass warm in my hand
as another hand
till January evaporates
quick as fumes from a bottle of solvent,
the sensation I tell you
titillating
as fingers skimming negligeed flesh,
the world falling into pleasure
too sensual to convey with words
composed

or whispered.

THE HOTEL HOT TUB

As the couple walks up to the rim of our tub,
five of us go still as mannequins, stare
at bogus dots in the distance, not one of us
shifting to make room.

They look to us
till we part our ring and hold
a collective breath.

When they squat, the man cries out
as if bone has broken or a limb
has come to life.

The woman flaunts gems
in her ears, around her neck, on several fingers
that stroke the man's cheek, his whole face
reflected in her eyes. Clearly,
she loves this bosomy man.

Hotel terraces light up. Tourists dressed for dinner
expect every good thing from a tropical night.
When the last swimmer climbs from the pool
only to gaze at it longingly, it is clear
part of her is still immersed.

A mother yoo-hoos her flock
from thirty flights over our heads.
I lean back. A dove's coo
rolls through each node of my spine.

The newcomers have too much to say

about money. Greed hangs in the air, haunts our tub
like algae.

I want to yell that no one
sitting in a hot tub on a warm beach in February
should long for more. Instead, I rise.
An extravagance of water drips free
but appreciation is intact, is a long red cape
I drag through sand
two shades lighter than beige.

Someone says, *ba-bye.*
I don't look back.

SMALL TOWN

When the mailman suggests I clip
the lavender that scrapes my office door
with its metal flap that opens
only for him, I refuse
to even *consider* it.

I tend to hold to what favors me.
To boughs pawing my windowpane.
To purple seeds on my sidewalk
like bits of gravel with no weight.

You see, I planted it from seed
and watched it curve its opulent way
through space till it fell
into place beside me.

Yet, Catholic-born, my guilt
has a way of gathering like possibility
or the downside of possibility: fear.
And the man is afraid of bees and lavender
pulses with bees. Yellow jackets, too.

So I clip. Some here. A little there.

Each twig chews
me out as I adjust its size and my attitude
stinks till stacks of pungent branches
litter my soft square of lawn.
The spiked odor of pruning like lemons
briny in my nose.

It will take time
to fill in the years but I'll learn to bend
with the limbs I left whole.

And like me, the shrub will have to find
new ways of reaching into the world
if it expects to grow.

And my mailman is less agitated
which, when you get right down to it,
is crucial to a writer.

HYDROLOGY

As far as my knowledge of hydrogen
extends, I understand little
flammable elements weigh next to nothing.

And colorless, odorless gas
combines chemically with oxygen.

Considering how complex it is
to fathom the science of water, I admit
what I want is simpler: A private pact
with sea. To slow my pace at its shore.
To see, as if for the first time, waves
pummel sand into rings
like compressed layers of an onion
once you slice through its rippled flesh.

El Niño—
All I know is rain
until my home feels like a cottage
inside a village
inside a toy globe filled with water.

And wind that howls,
head flung back. Air in February
warmer than we can expect from May,
it's rhododendron rush,
irises waiting.

When spring recaptures sun and forsythia
flares yellow, we won't remember
network flashes of homes giving way,

rooftops pried apart, couch and chimney
drifting down river. Or cliffs
like ones that hold up our town
sliding into the ocean like mud,
no like gravel
from plates of glass.

BICYCLING THE BAJA PENINSULA

All morning
we pedal side by side
with an orange left between us to eat.
A Mexican orange, size of a plum.
My fingers clench it like ribs
holding lungs in place, turn it
over and over, precious
nut in my claws.

When I finally peel the rind, thirst
wide as the desert before and behind
mounts in my throat the way dread can build
in the center of me.

Feeling foolish, *gringo-ish,*
I walk to the center of the road, flag a car
as if a race is about to begin.

The driver assures
food is a couple of miles away.
I take a *couple* to mean *two.*
My ears infer what my stomach can bear.

We ride four miles
then five then ten
through a dozen valleys
far from green.

I curse that man,
mistrust in his eyes, as light fades and hunger
squeezes my insides shut.

I ride on as the worst, most discontent
version of myself.

Finally, coasting into a village
studded with lights more splendid
than stars, pastels shine and my eyes
eye food. Peppers strung over stucco.
Tomatoes springing from clay.

In spite of breathlessness, I pick up the speed
of my desire till *frijoles* and tortillas
dissolve on my tongue
as much as longing for anything more
than night now was: A cup of cool water.
A warm tent on a warm beach.

THE CARPENTER

A few queries into our interview
he says, *I love all God has blessed me with:*
my wife, four sons, four daughters.

I thought, *I can't write about him.*
Life like this doesn't belong to me.

On his acreage it seems little
is elsewhere. Homes
to house a sister, mother, in-laws.
No member of his family lives
in the absence of another.

Compared to most I meet,
the me, me, me of them,
he is selfless.

Still, there is little link between us.
Childless by choice, I have no family
within a thousand miles, no interest
in Christianity, its callings. I believe
responsible men father only one child.
Maybe two.

We speak across chasms.

I can't say what, exactly, but something
I neither see nor touch
warms me.

When I walk away

under clouds raining gray over town,
the sky feels lighter than before.

WATER DISH

The cat's water dish is covered in ash
fallen from the mill stack west of town,
a monument of brick that rears
over the bay, a pillar of toxicity
no one talks about.
As if yoga, festivals, and eating
organic makes air faultless, noxious gas
breathable.

I wipe out the bowl
gooey with soot, remember
hearing my cat's sex life last night.
A howl from deep within her body
belly-up. No complexity
to her love story.

For that moment, I froze.
Beyond that,
nothing. No yelling from me
would make that cat roll over
and pull up her panties.

When I got up to spy,
two pairs of eyes glowed in the dark
like burning cigarettes.

I shooed away the tomcat.
Picked up my harlot,
heart pounding against the cave of her ribs.
Each nail of her claw kneading my chest.
Sting. Prickle. Sting.

I lingered...

When I slipped back into bed
my husband stirred and I settled
myself into comfort
more my size.

LOOKING FOR SWANSONVILLE
—for Marcelle

I veer off Beaver Valley Road
in search of your new home.
Our friendship spans ten years
so no way I'll let us fade
fast as your last address.

I roll down my window,
let the scent of valley in, the green
I swear, greener than in town.

With no hum of traffic I hear
each detail specific to air.

Right turn by a one-room church.

I pass easily into homes you choose:
tiny apartment by the courthouse,
log house on Hastings,
sailboat tied stem to mooring.
Though I missed one, the year you remarried
and our friendship divorced. No reason
we should have gone silent. But there
we were all the same.

Now, a farm. A refuge
that sheds the weight of me
bored with town, tourists, egos
keeping score. Here, no muss
to edit, no fear of losing time.

When we walk your garden
hay-covered and swelling with lettuce, beans,
radishes (I didn't know grew underground),
I think this is where you'll dig in
adding years to the heap of compost
that holds heat like a furnace, life
in its hands, ones firm enough
to hold you together.

HIDDEN POOLS
—Tucson, Arizona

I.

I love the way cicada hiss
before a monsoon
swallows us whole
as the lie I tell myself
when I say I don't *need* to return here
to balance my rainy life with warmth.

When an oriole, lush orange on black,
lands on a bough of Saguaro, it weighs
on my affections.
How the contrast startles:
pert, soft feathers
against prickly limbs a hundred years old,
hollow of moisture so deep inside
I imagine it sleeps.

Come dusk. I sip beer through a slice of lime
till sun clears the last tile roof. Firmly
night displaces day.

Now, the winter I came for. Evenings warm like you
wouldn't believe.

II.

In a yard dry as chalk dust,
a sprinkler line erupts. A thin stream
rushes over gasping earth,
unrestrained, merciful
in the absolute way it matters.
Two quail, regal as majorettes,

summon their flock. Other birds
descend, hopping transfixed, wise
to the speed of evaporation.

A fluke of survival not to be missed.
A length of hose riddled with holes
extending life
solely by coincidence.

THE WASHING

She doesn't bother
to look in the mirror
to search her roots for gray
before calling the salon

the way she would
when her husband was still alive.
When she still fixed a meal
eagerly. When she still cooked
at all.

How she misses his caress.
Much like her hairdresser
massages her head.
Slow, rhythmical strokes,
washing her hair once
maybe twice a week,
knowing just how gently to pull
each short strand gleaming wet.

She doesn't specify a particular stylist
preferring one method
expectantly over another.

She needs all the gals
for ballast, their fingers to touch
her like a timid lover.

To remind her
how it feels to resemble someone

living. Someone who hasn't slipped away
unseen, concealed

by so much loss.

MIAMI BEACH

All I do is stare
mutely at the girl by the beach-side grocery.
Ragged clothing. Left foot with missing toes
like a gap between teeth. Moon-white eyes
in the midnight of her skin.

In one week I learn to distinguish
Cuban from Haitian, this girl
from ones who speak enough English
to clean hotel rooms, who stand in white shirtwaists
waiting for the bus.

People hurry past us to buy beer,
cream to protect their skin from the sun it seeks,
inflatable plastic to keep kids afloat.

Behind me, a woman smirks,
reminds me of the mom on *Jerry Seinfeld*,
whine in her voice, aqua-net hair,
clear sheet of vinyl I suppose covers her couch.
When she spits at the girl whose head hangs down,
whose whole body acquiesces I think,
my god it's true, the most oppressed
oppress the most.

Now, police prod the girl into a van.
Fear, raw as a welt on her face,
routs her inside out.
She vomits onto their shoes.

I close my eyes
to see
this girl
adrift on a makeshift raft,
searching an ocean for a high-rise reef.
Cane fields across the Atlantic.
Machete slashing her toe.
Catalogue in her lap, all the things
she wants to have.

As for me: I'm not hardened
by these fringey streets, cannot pass
obliviously, still know bigotry
when I see it, still find much
of myself
in the girl who left
one sandal behind.

DECEMBER

We stand under a full moon
to lose ourselves in the white
disk of silence

my friend blames for heat
rising in her, for cramps and bleeding,
for striking out at her husband with a fist
of tension clenching her chest.

At a time like this
it's right to walk downtown
to the pub where beer is made in a wide metal vat
I thought, at first, was a furnace
steaming to heat those of us gathered at the bar.
When I lay my hands on the cool, lathed wood,
it warms.

On a winter night, it's good to bathe
oneself in conversation, in a friend's dread
of hormones if that's what she needs, in hops
brewing behind us. Less so

in a tourist's string of questions:
where to eat, where to stay, where to go
tomorrow when we must work
and he slips out of town by ferry
in a rig nearly
the size of my home—

our town with its mill smoke
blossoming, already blurred by memory,
distance, or fog

CAL'S BEACH

Waiting for my bicycle
to be healed, one flat tire
and a missing spoke, I walk
to where a cove of sand
meets sea.

Galoshes on.
Hour to kill.
I wade in.

Each wave
against my rubbery feet
sounds like the light
touch of a woman's hand
on the bus last night,
week before Christmas

houses sporting lights
like sequins
released over rooftops
in long twinkling webs.

The woman held a newborn
under a pale blue blanket
gold-metallic threads
woven through.

When the baby squirmed
she unwrapped his body,
patted his tiny, delicate back

gently

the way mothers do.

UNSPOKEN

My father slides his belt
backward through each loop.
Leather wound around his palm.
Slack primed to strike.

Under a canopy of grapevines
I struggle against anger
equaling my own. I grab the strap.
You can imagine how that went over.

A stubborn man, a headstrong girl—
two tempers in full dress.

I remember running, halting, turning
dead on to face him.
How he stood breathless, the smoker he was.
How fear filled me with will.

I swung the belt, the world terrifying
and safely my own
at once.

This August day,
the sound of leather snapping
in rage comes back to me as I shake out a towel
just dry off the line.

After years of living
where rain runs into rivers,
rivers into sound, sound into straits,
all of it whirling into the arms of sea

I realize why he and I never mention that day
flagrant as sun in our eyes.
Why some truths are better left alone
to flow unobstructed
to the far reaches of memory
companioned only by weightless things:
sound, air, light,
forgiveness.

THE VISIT

I travel by air to visit my father. Odd
how one can race at the speed of sound
and be in no hurry.

If you are from Chicago, Boston, or New York,
if your parents prospered, chances are
you'll impose on them one winter in Florida
where January skies
do not close in on you.

When the plane touches down,
my feet won't fit into shoes.
So, bloated toes staring up, I walk
barefoot through the gate into eyes
of disapproval, die a little as my father leans
but does not hug, his white shirt glowing
against the tan on his neck and face
it, no matter how we try, restraint quashes us,
the moment a winter night in Maine, air in me
so cold it burns.

At dinner, my dad's hair, white
as the loaf of bread we share, saddens me
more than gray strands stiff in my own
or how little we share of each other
aside from furrows between our brows,
compact bodies, tempers that claw
like tomcats when we are wronged.

I sleep in a room too gingham
for a concrete condo ascending

a tropical shore. Keyed up, I step out
on a deck four flights above sand.
Behind me, through sliding glass,
my father and his new wife watch television.
A western. Cowboys gather in a saloon.

I try to name the shade of gulf sea.
A color postcards display, tourists expect
for their money and status
is a view of it
lapping a beach
sea walls define.

BROMELIAD

When you water
this stemless cousin of pineapple
privileged in its snazzy clay pot,

fill each leaf
cupped upward
like hands of a saint
to hold moisture between rains.

Watch how the wet drips down
to satisfy the hidden bulb.
A process so pure.

Now, think back to a time
when your cultivated *heart of flame*
blossomed its fist of red
deep in the hollow of a banyan tree.
And what drops the massive limbs could spare
trickled to thirsty fronds
pent in a berth of moss.

This is what I imagine
in my bathrobe on Saturday mornings.
Motown turned up and down-
filled slippers on my feet

as I quench my bromeliad
arcing a delicate stream
or spurting

corresponding to my patience,
the slant of my pour.

WAITING FOR NANCY
—Tugan, Australia

I.
North of Cairns
daylight bristles skin
like leaning into an oven will
or holding a burning match too long.

Daily, I cut through my dread of roaches
trying to make some piece of fear
fit.

As for the ocean, an invitation of blue.
But beneath its calm surface, a city
of sea wasps.

II.
We pack, move south, swim
at last without safety nets, send postcards
boasting sand and sea.

Mornings, no Kookaburra wakes us,
flirty with laughter, or fruit bats chattering, chattering—
but this is the Australia we left home for.

III.
When sun abandons sky it leaves
an ocean to mourn itself.
We light candles, store water, hold hands
to form a singleness to our worry.

On the radio, men name the hurricane *Nancy*,
sure only a woman's wrath
could whip a beach into craters,
cause trees to lean as if ready to heave,
drive parakeets, usually giddy and bold,
to fall silent.

I move our things to the highest shelf.
Fear one of us drowning in a swirling wave, the other
in loneliness.

Raised to believe in the sign of the cross,
I join mind and heart to each breast, try to pray
like my mother prays, patiently as one
chisels stone.

SHE WEARS EARRINGS
INTO THE SHOWER

Earrings intact, Jane Fonda
steps from the shower
in a film where she plays a drunk
and, we're led to believe, a murderess.

Now, completely off this subject,
though I promise to tie things together
the way actors do in a call back. You see
my husband thinks of me as a prototype: a woman
who lives how women live
and when *I* shower I remove my earrings

and because it takes only one
knot in a string of familiarities to throw him, he asks
why she wore earrings *into* the shower.

Bemused, I watch the rest of the film in silence,
a life story perched beyond my reach.

Later, I ask him to name three things
he thinks of when he thinks of women.
Hesitation roams limb to limb.
He is scared our words will breeze
into a gale.

OK, he says, *tears, how easily they come on.*
And it's true when he tries to fix my fears
like a leak in the roof, I can cry
in frustration before going over it again:
what women want, require, long for
is empathy not help!

Next he adds, *intuition*. My internal scale,
I suppose, that works to balance two lives
with devotion between them.

When he offers the word *breasts*
like a gag-gift, he admits
they hardly warrant nicknames
in a way that conjures my sense of humor back
from where it was hiding. And, finally,
with arms extended so we might finish this conversation
unwounded, he says, *earrings.*
You can bet they wear earrings.

SUNSET AT NORTH BEACH
—for the neophytes

There is so much to love
about summer in the Northwest
that, frankly, I don't know where to begin.

What you *must* do when warmth lingers
into dusk, is eat dinner outside

best if freshly mown grass
swamps your toes and a cat
sprawls on your heat-soaked lap.

If, at nine o'clock,
daylight still beams, tie up your hair
and head for the beach north of town
to see the end of day slip into sea.

If you're anything like me
you'll sit until the sun,
no longer round,
grows slight but unfaded.

When you turn your head you'll see little
by way of distraction but a dog
nosing the beach, teenagers
curled round each other. A couple
rising to walk on.

This is when it's best to stay.
To relish the steady swish of waves
lapping waves as the world pauses
for a moment, leaving you

in awe, unable to speak.
When you finally stand
to fling sand from the seat of your pants,
it's because you feel too much
unforgiving in the crisp air off the Straits
suspended between what was merely chilly
to your skin and the downright cold
I promise
summer or no summer
comes next.

ABOUT THE AUTHOR

Craving Water: Poems of Ordinary Life in a Northwest Village is Sanelli's sixth collection of poetry. Her poems have been published widely in journals and anthologies.

She has contributed essays and cover stories to *The Seattle Times, Northwest Palate Magazine,* and *Northwest Woman Magazine.* Her commentaries have been aired on Northwest Public Radio and NPR. They are heard weekly on KSER FM; and monthly on KONP AM. Her column, *A Writer's Notebook,* appears monthly in Port Townsend's newspaper *The Leader.*

Honorariums include an Artist Trust GAP Award, A Jack Straw Writers Award, The Skagit River Poetry Festival, The Seattle Poetry Festival, The Seattle Bumbershoot Festival, a 2003 writing residency in Costa Rica, and an upcoming writing residency at Fundacion Valparaiso, Spain.

She presents her work extensively throughout the country.

HOW WE GOT OUR NAME
from Pleasure Boat Studio

an essay written by Ouyang Xiu,
Song Dynasty poet, essayist, and scholar,
on the twelfth day of the twelfth month
in the renwu year (January 25, 1043)

"I have heard of men of antiquity who fled from the world to distant rivers and lakes and refused to their dying day to return. They must have found some source of pleasure there. If one is not anxious for profit, even at the risk of danger, or is not convicted of a crime and forced to embark; rather, if one has a favorable breeze and gentle seas and is able to rest comfortably on a pillow and mat, sailing several hundred miles in a single day, then is boat travel not enjoyable? Of course, I have no time for such diversions. But since 'pleasure boat' is the designation of boats used for such pastimes, I have now adopted it as the name of my studio. Is there anything wrong with that?"

Translated by Ronald Egan